TO YŪGEN, WITH LOVE

Anushree Warrier

BookLeaf Publishing

India | USA | UK

Presentation by *BookLeaf Publishing*

Web: www.bookleafpub.com

E-mail: info@bookleafpub.com

ISBN: 9789358361964

First edition 2021

To the people who are my universe, to the people who are alive in

this universe, and to the people whose spirits live on in this

universe, I dedicate this book to you.

Yūgen (幽玄) is a Japanese word that translates to a profound,
mysterious sense of the beauty of this universe, and the sad beauty
of human suffering

ACKNOWLEDGEMENTS

Thank you, Mummy & Daddy – for everything. One lifetime feels too short to love you back the way you love me. You are my lifelines. My world. My core.

Thank you, Sankar – for being my perfect intruder, for tolerating all of me, and for celebrating us. The magic of your love made this possible.

Thank you, Ravichettan – for watching over me from some corner of this universe. You always inspired me to head on with a song on my lips and hope in my heart, and that is what I will continue to do. Shoorpi continues to tease me on your behalf too. :)

Thank you, Amma & Achchan – somewhere, our paths were meant to cross, and I am so lucky they did. Thank you, for your care and encouragement.

Thank you, my beautiful Aunts and Uncles – for cheering me on all throughout, and for pampering me more than I have ever deserved.

Thank you, my dearest cousins, and in-laws – you are the closest siblings I have ever had. Your love and laughter are my driving force.

Thank you, my tiny nieces, and nephews – I try so hard to be your cool aunt, but you are way too cool for me.

Thank you to all my teachers, bosses, and mentors – for blessing me with your constant guidance and silent motivation.

To all my music and dance gurus, thank you for teaching me to put my heart and soul into all that I do.

Lucky are those who have their biggest cheerleaders in their friends. To all my closest friends, peers, and well-wishers, thank you for your unwavering and irreplaceable presence in my life.

A huge thank you to the Bookleaf publishing team. There I was, wasting away my talents, when you silently popped up on my Instagram advertisements. And here we are, one book later. Thank you for rekindling the belief that this dream, too, was possible.

And most importantly, thank you, to my dear beloved readers – for picking this book up and for joining along on this crazy journey of mine. The characters in many of the poems are purely imaginary (some human, and some not), allowing me the opportunity to weave different perspectives together. Some poems are dedications to the people I love, and some are messages of hope. I hope they resonate with you at some level, warm you up to the feeling that you are not alone in the darkness and assure you that the universe is celebrating every moment that you are alive. I hope and pray that in the darkest of times, you find the strength to believe in the beauty of all things beautiful and painful in this universe - your yūgen.

PREFACE

You see, there is little about this book

that I can tell.

They hold slices of my journey,

from every nook,

straight from the soul,

none written to sell.

Some real, some imaginary,

some personal, much ordinary.

This book does offer

strange characters,

some hard realities,

some truths softer.

Just like the ways of the universe,

it has no specific plot,

why, even, would this be a book, then?

I know not.

Each thought, each poem,

allowed me the room,

to step into imaginary shoes,

to savour the mystery,

to cherish the wonder,

and befriend the gloom.

As words flowed,

I wrote.

The more I wrote,

more words flowed.

I am in awe of all things in this universe.

Of limitless skies,

rooted grounds,

lacklustre eyes,

nature's sounds.

Of stars twinkling,

the light calling,

clouds rumbling,

the sun shining,

the good, bad, and ugly,

the people we hold snugly,

the yin and yang,

and all that came from the big bang.

All of it,

that this preface can never fit.

This sense of deep wonder –

in hope, in love, in light,

has helped me wander,

befriend the darkness,

and defend the night.

The Japanese call this beauty the *Yūgen,*

although, for some, this too, might seem mundane.

Through these poems,

my silence found a sound.

In that what I thought was lost,

my heart and soul were found.

For now, I shall hold on to hope,

hold on to my beloved yūgen,

that I so deeply have begun to treasure,

all over again.

Through these stories

I bring to you – promise –

in hope, in love, in light.

For, deep within you, there is might,

of which, I pray that you never lose sight.

To Yūgen, With Love

1.   MY STORY...

When I think of my story,

this beautiful journey comes to mind.

The perfect end to which,

I shall never find.

Some highs, some blows,

some yeses, some noes.

lots of laughter, boughs of woes.

Some constants,

with intentions well-defined.

Some deviants,

their roles, perhaps, not well-aligned.

Some step in as a boon,

some leave too soon,

some stay on to become chapters,

short, long, even ever-afters.

Some leave behind beautiful memories,

And some, vague, unnerving histories.

I am on that page of my story –

where the ties are strange and the mind, weary.

Yet, the heart yearns for companions,

ones that are averse to treachery.

I shall neither impose on you,

nor add to your worry.

But, with all my heart, if I may ask –

Would you be a chapter in my story?

2.   MY TWO JEWELS...

Two people held me first,

propped me up, calmed my rants,

straightened my pants,

and walked me to school.

They stood by me and warmed my hands,

while I trotted along, playing all cool

They know me in and out,

they know my core – without a doubt.

They have run to my aid, caught me pout,

and pulled me back into the right route.

They have never once forced upon me any rules.

For years later, when I chose "my man",

they smiled at my unplanned plan,

and called us both "fools"!

They have shown me the way to my senses,

and taught me life's golden lessons.

I am in awe of such glow and grace,

in their merry songs and joyful ways,

without a line of defeat on their face,

at any low point along life's maze.

Bless their courage to smile – their biggest tool.

All these years that have gone by,

they still stand by me, warm my hands,

while I trot along, playing all cool.

To all the mothers and fathers,

who gift us our wings,

and the liberty to fly.

I write this, in your honour,

with tears of joy.

3.   A PAIR OF SLIPPERS AND A FEW COINS

Every night, I watch him counting his last few coins.

Lighting a fire to warm his fingertips,

shifting uncomfortably on a bed of dead leaves,

embracing the lone night's cold, unkind heaves.

I thank the moon for keeping him silent company,

for tucking him in,

away from this world and its raging cacophony.

At dawn, we pedal away.

A few milk bags left to give away.

Some more coins he thus, earns.

Knowing these would hardly break bread,

his stomach churns.

With a lone rag and a shoe polish,

he sits, barefooted, outside the parish.

As the day passes, I watch him smile

at the sheen on others' boots,

watching another daydream, perhaps,

of a life from soot to suits.

As dusk invites the end of yet another day,

I sense his feeling of despair,

his shivers and quivers.

He moves aimlessly in search of one more coin,

like a mother searching for a child that was never hers.

He is hungry now,

desperate for a few grains.

I drag him to those garbage bins,

and he smiles at the sight of rotten bread.

To dine like this,

I wonder about his past-sins.

The cold night looms in

with a question mark on our sorrows,

he throws the last few coins on my worn-out face,

seeking answers.

But oh dear, Master,

I am just a pair of slippers,

and you, a poor old cobbler,

yesterday, today, and for all of tomorrow.

4.   AND THE FAIRY WALKED AWAY...

Once upon a time, lived Santa and the tooth fairy.

They ruled my bedtime stories and erased thoughts scary.

To kings and princes belonged many glorious tales,

while princesses and orphans stayed locked up in jails.

Fables with sweet endings put me to sleep.

The evil was destroyed, only goodwill and wonder to keep.

One fine day, the window threw open,

and a violent storm raged in.

I had suddenly become a grown woman

and life's harsh realities claimed their win.

I looked into my mother's eyes,

how her masked fairy tales were given away.

And when I stepped into the world outside,

the Santa and the tooth fairy had walked away.

5.   THE MATTER OF BELONGINGNESS

Far across in a distant land,

lying down for hours together,

cushioned in the desert sand,

I counted every star I could gather.

My camera lay next to me –

still, calm, peaceful.

Though this was my n^{th} tour,

the $(n+1)^{th}$ always felt more beautiful.

I would speak to my folks back home

every single day.

We argued about my confusing postal addresses,

this in April, that in May.

Sigh.

Strange. I sensed a feeling that was brewing.

Was it homesickness, that I was nonchalantly masking?

In search of my passion,

I had moved continents,

Yet here we now were.

My soul craved for a home,

over a camera's shutter?

What was this feeling,

oddly brewing?

Was the sun, back home,

ever so beautiful when it rose?

Were the nights, back home,

lonelier than the path I chose?

So many photographs I had captured in the last two decades,

none matched the memories of home and its various shades.

Countless landscapes, myriad faces,

wouldn't soothe the pain of missing family on many days.

Did they ever map my travel?

Or follow my published photographs?

Or miss my presence?

My mailbox full of unsent drafts.

Sigh.

Slowly, time flew fly,

and a year went by.

Overruled by "the feeling",

I wrapped my winding travels,

for my soul needed much unravelling.

Now, here I am,

lying on the grass for hours together.

Trying to count the infinite stars,

home-made brownie points for the more I could gather.

Surrounded by folks on our picnic mattress,

laughing merrily, clinking our glasses.

Indescribable, this feeling of oneness

Perhaps, it was a matter of belongingness.

6.   A LAND WITHOUT BORDERS

Outside the window,

the night was dark,

the roads deserted,

and the dogs did not bark.

Mother's bedtime stories

had me all tucked in,

yet I feigned sleep,

knowing that the din would begin.

And begin it did,

the silent night resonated

with sudden blasts and screams.

The moonlight, now, blurred,

by smoke and shards, in streams.

Prayers we all started chanting,

Minutes to go before they hit us,

but we were still counting.

I did not know how and when I fell asleep.

Strange, this escape felt,

as sleep came deep.

When I opened my eyes,

I saw one vast desert,

no screaming, no cries.

Only a sea of people

happy, chattering sounds.

Oh, in that vista of colours,

I could forever drown.

But I ran ahead,

looking for mother, worried.

The smoke had vanished,

and sadness buried.

There, I spotted her,

examining a pair of shiny sandals.

Oh, why was she laughing,

her hand full of yellow bangles?

She shouted out to me,

"Oh, dear darling, we are free. Run. Play.

The big men resolved all differences,

this is where we shall now stay.

No more borders, not one barrier

Some differences, sure,

but we shall be alive and merrier.

Oh, go, make new friends now.

Our lives can have new endings, now.

This new world can teach us new things,

with people kinder and more humane beings.

Will you, my baby, promise to embrace this new land?

Will you, my darling, respect those with whom you stand?

Just imagine, love, this land without borders, not one barrier,

we can be humans, finally. One for all and all for the merrier"

I skipped and hopped,

hungry to soak all this in — the sights and sounds.

I would die to be on this land,

where love and joy knew no bounds.

No more fights,

None without reason,

No more cries,

No more treason...

Boom!

A flash of light and another blast.

Mother's bangles shattered.

Her eyes open, aghast

at the sight of children's bodies battered.

My eyes threw open

I was jolted back

Was all this just a dream?

For, when I opened my eyes,

the night was silent again,

not one smile, not one scream.

There he was – my father lay dead,

and my brother slowly falling through the window…

I was being left behind an orphan,

and my mother was bleeding–to–death, a widow.

No.

I will not be left alone in this cruel world.

Full of evils and mindless disorder.

I ran towards the window.

Before I knew it,

one bullet, then two.

I smiled,

as I fell back into my dream –

into that land without borders.

7.   OH, DEAR TIME...

Oh, dear time, what shall I ask of you?

Some strength to smile,

when you make me feel blue?

Or to ground me like a magnet,

when happiness is due?

At the finish line,

I hope that the smiles are many,

and the maladies few,

that beyond the dark, grey clouds,

soothing sunshine awaits in queue.

After all, oh, dear time,

you and I, are we not friends, too?

Now, walking towards your end,

every heartbeat feels true,

Every lesson you have taught me,

too dear to bid adieu to.

Perhaps, dear time, in all these years,

I may have outgrown you…

8.   CLARION CALL

I watched as the rains poured down the windowpane,

flashes of lightning mimicked my searing pain.

I walked out of the room, slowly, unaware of my being

the thunderous roar slicing through my numb feeling.

The afternoon felt so dark,

I could see a world no more.

My life had no sky, no sea, no shore.

I looked at the doctor's report –

How could this happen to me?

A tumour was to become my endgame.

I had no time, no aim.

There was no time left, to aim.

Dark clouds gathered around to hound me.

As if, my fate had been sealed already.

I had streets to cross before I reached the bay.

Or I could just lunge forward and end this day.

Just then, a wind snatched my report away.

Suddenly, my hands were empty,

and my gloomy fate on paper was taken away.

I felt my legs cross the streets,

towards the bay,

with my mind prompting me onward,

to mark this day.

The clouds had begun to clear away,

and a shy silent sun had begun to make way.

I had to stay on track,

there was still time to bid adieu to

I had to befriend my leftover life,

and focus on what was left to do.

I was an artist.

I knew what I had to do –

just cut out the noise,

and paint without further ado.

With my brushes and my canvas,

I painted for hours – of a bridge standing tall,

strong, resolute, and unfailing –

all because of a roaring clarion call.

This became my favourite painting,

my defining all–time highest selling.

It has been three years since,

the sun always emerges from the clouds, like a true born prince.

Today, when the rain pours down the windowpane,

I fear no clouds, I embrace the pain.

Gone are those days,

when darkness was be–all–end–all.

Now I create my own sunshine,

I simply follow my clarion call.

9. THE PERFECT INTRUDER

When I did not expect,

I hardly hoped for a perfect prospect.

When my hopes of finding love lay astray,

I assumed that the person I want,

was either neigh or far away.

Separated by time, fate, and distance,

I found cheap thrills in waiting –

some strange, brave, sixth sense.

And just when I found myself least expectant,

in walked a prospect,

like some already existing descendant.

Completely floored by this intruder,

distance, time – did not matter.

When nothing mattered

but those moments of being swept off my feet,

I fell for that intruder, over and over, repeat.

The wedding happened, simple and pious,

with the promise of a marriage love-filled and joyous.

Ever since, little things and everyday

have become symbols of true, mad, and deep love.

And I keep thanking myself for waiting –

for my perfect intruder, for my dearest white dove.

10. REMEMBERING HIM...

From the day you were born

until the day you had to go,

a thousand people you got to know.

A thousand lives you touched,

left behind a million memories,

for friends and foe, did you know?

The way you ran home to play with me,

the way you pulled my leg with glee,

the way you lifted me off my feet,

the way you made my joys meet.

The way I stood by the gate waiting for you,

my eyes scrutinizing every person, vehicle, and schoolbag too.

Every hour that went by I would count – one, two, …

None matched the joy of spending time with you.

The way I watched you study for your exams,

for your absence, I had to pay that price.

The way you took every step,

with such gentle perfection,

On every life that you touched,

you showered selfless affection.

How I envied your dedication, devotion,

with such admiration.

To learn all this from you,

 "life" was too short a duration.

The way we talked and talked,

until our voices went sore,

of music, travel, food, and so much more.

Your stories took me to a world of ideals,

made me believe that perfection existed.

A world of "fantasy" that I could only dream of,

one where kindness and generosity meant all.

The way your shoulders shook when you laughed,

the way you frowned when in worry,

the way you washed your feet time and again,

the way you tidied everything up, never in fury.

The way you had a solution to every problem in life,

the way you carried your aura – ahead of your time.

The way you shone like the rarest of rare gems,

compassionate, jovial, fun-loving, bright, and yet, so sublime.

The way you would call me,

trick me with fake hellos,

calm me down,

in all my highs and lows.

I know I can never hear or see that again,

for now, in a place far away,

you stand strong, holding my hands,

and backing me up, however mellow.

Today I look back at the thirty—one years of my life,

twenty—five with you, and the rest without you.

Each second reminds me, painfully,

of how much I miss you.

From time, I often beg some strength,

to feel your presence,

to accept this reality

that I can never see or hear you,

to help me wear a smile and

take a step, always thinking of you.

Time seems endless as every second we mourn.

My dear darling brother,

I cannot believe that you are gone.

I do not want to. I never will. You are here.

Right here. Right here. Right here.

11. THE TOUCH OF YOUR HAND

I drifted into nothingness,

the black hole had sucked the living soul out of me.

I screamed and screamed.

Somebody, stop me from falling.

Somebody, set me free.

Who I thought was immortal, was not?

What I thought was permanent, was not.

With you gone, our 'Forever' became 'never again',

and my heart formed a million irreversible knots.

Tears streamed down my fluffy cheeks,

bit through my faith,

swept my happiness away, and

killed my hope.

No more letters,

no more calls.

In one corner lay an unwanted telephone,

in another, your last envelope.

I lost you, your jokes,

I lost us, our words,

Will I find you in the smell on your shirts?

Or in your sounds resonating in my ears?

Futile, is it, yearning for your hands to brush through mine?

Pointless, is it, waiting for your fingers to intertwine with mine?

For those moments when our eyes meet in glory to shine?

For those moments when your touch feels purer than a shrine?

For so many hearts and souls,

you were water and you were the land.

But it took you less than a second

to slip away like sand.

I am now a lost soul forever,

staring into emptiness,

desperate, for the touch of your hand.

12. FAITH

The sun rises, and a life is born.

In beam joys and divine words are sworn.

An organism becomes a whole human being,

and we are ejected into this world, alive and kicking.

Soon, we are lured into the mysteries of mythologies and lords.

A particular he-who-must-always-be-named will help even all odds.

The longer the morrows and stranger the sorrows,

strength from our loved ones we begin to borrow.

Days, weeks, months, and years that follow,

life, with its kicks and blows, begins to seem hollow.

In time, we realize that humanity it is,

that eventually matters,

that which deceives, stands by or shatters.

Is it all an illusion, then?

This belief in a "God",

Is it for real or some clickbait,

this faith?

How can believers, then, be such extremists?

How can teachings so pure produce such sadists?

If you are all-knowing, oh God,

grace us with your presence.

Give us a shout-out,

perhaps, give us a nod?

Oh, wait, are you acting through us?

Or maybe, just maybe, are you somewhere within us?

Sometimes, I have faith —

in the magic of the universe.

in the reason for living

in the reason for being

in love and kindness.

Is this the same faith that will strengthen my mould?

Is this the same faith that could rule this world?

13. A DREAM OF DREAMS

She quipped, "I always have dreams",

I smiled, "tell me the best of all your dreams".

She looked at me with a strange expression,

as if holding on to a desire that would never attain fruition.

While I humoured her,

she continued to be lost in her deep thoughts.

I watched her face, her focused eyes,

and tried to fathom those entangled knots.

She exclaimed, "I saw, saw a dream.

One where all my dreams come true,

and my reality was the dream."

Her words sent a pang down my throat,

as I peered into her bowl of coins and tattered piece of cloth.

Her wondrous smile moistened my eyes,

and I whispered to her, "One day you will rise."

With longing, despair, innocence, and hunger,

she looked right at the neighbouring beggar.

"Until then, I will save my dreams.

And who knows, one day,

I could have a reality bigger than any of my dreams?"

I hugged her, my soul wanting to scream.

I remembered something I was once told.

Lucky are those who live their dreams,

luckier are those, who can dare to dream.

14. LOST ...

HER

It was a day darker than the rest,

rife with gloom, at life's behest.

Walking along a deserted path, all forlorn,

I realized more than ever before that I was so alone.

I walked and walked, twists, and turns, lanes and by-lanes,

my silent sorrow leading me past unknown windowpanes.

Disoriented I was, perhaps, too lost in time and life,

to notice myself following a pair of feet – firmer than mine.

The man's silhouette seemed purposeful, so affirmative.

Call it impulse, but I followed him, unaware of self or motive.

He crossed roads, highways, streets, people,

silently I followed.

All chaos subdued,

as if conquered by tranquillity,

my roars mellowed.

Should I have reached out?

Told him I was right behind, asked him to remain?

His proximity was my solace.

this alien feeling too strong to retain.

But, before I knew where he would lead me to,

I reached this place I call home.

My destination, though, was now new.

He walked on, never realizing that I had fallen,

fallen out of my sorrow.

following him, his footsteps,

his presence leading me to a new morrow.

And then I turned away, empty and sore,

to a road that led me to my home,

with another incomplete story,

my soul more lost than ever before.

HIM

It was a day darker than the rest,

rife with gloom, at life's behest.

Walking along a deserted path, all forlorn,

I realized more than ever before that I was so alone.

I walked and walked, twists, and turns, lanes and by-lanes,

my silent sorrow leading me past unknown windowpanes.

Disoriented I was, perhaps, too lost in time and life,

to notice a pair of innocent lost feet following mine.

Her shadow seemed to crave for direction,

her low sighs yearned for someone's affection.

I went on ahead,

and her footsteps followed mine.

Silently we crossed streetlights and houses astray,

her presence growing on me,

the darkness in my life slowly ebbing away.

Should I have turned around?

Told her I was right there, asked her to remain?

Her proximity was my solace,

this alien feeling too pure to restrain.

But, before I knew where the roads led us to,

her shadow paused uncomfortably

and turned away without further ado.

Unbeknownst to her, I had fallen,

out of my darkness, into the light with her.

Tears streaming down my eyes, I wobbled ahead,

Lost again, my heart, a silent massacre.

15. THE FLASHLIGHT

With silent strength, I tread along lone boulevards.

Nothing no longer catches me off guard,

nothing no longer seems off the cards.

On a lone night like this,

I had been brutally raped.

My genitals neither spared,

nor left to be saved.

Many mocked me,

some stifled my unheard cries,

but I felt more deceived,

by people and their insensible lies.

For some, I was out at the wrong time.

For some, it was the wrong season.

Some said I would lose anyways,

my fight had no compelling reason.

Despite all the chaos,

I searched for eyes that mattered,

looks that reassured my soul,

and spirits unshattered.

Many attempts to break the mantle I mustered,

somehow, made my resolve stronger,

despite a mind that was way beyond flustered.

Much time has since passed,

I am braver now, less naïve.

I am no princess. I am my own knight.

I find solace in my own truth.

Pleading for my spirit's worth, from booth to booth.

I have found the courage to head on in my fight.

It has taken me years though, but I will lead with light.

There is no oasis for me, you see.

So, all I can do, is cross this rough sea.

I am a victim of YOUR sons' barbaric deeds,

your judgement, your hypocrisy, and your rotten seeds.

You cannot kill my undying spirit.

Even though I know you wish they did.

I will not let myself lose sight.

I will not let you to stop my fight.

Your wrong cannot win over my right.

Your darkness cannot tarnish my flashlight.

15. I WAS FOUR, HE WAS THREE...

I saw him playing on the street,

I was four and he was three.

I went up to him and asked if I could join.

Not knowing how our futures would entwine.

He considered for a moment,

and then burst into a glorious smile,

In our play, laughter, smiles and cries,

we have been inseparable, all this while.

He would never come to school with me.

His father sent him to another one.

I would ask him about his school friends,

but he would just break into a frenzied run.

Today, I am twelve, he is eleven.

Only playmates now, we hardly share a thing.

Something does seem amiss at his school though,

he seems to be hiding something.

After school today, I shall ask if he wants to talk things out,

he seemed the most disturbed last evening, without a doubt.

I packed my bags, waiting for the school bell to ring,

But just then, I heard an explosion – loud and deafening.

As I scurried out of the classroom to find a hiding place,

I bumped into a huge man with a masked face.

He pinned me against the wall,

and slapped me hard with all the hatred.

Then, he looked up and smiled at his God,

as if the deed was the most sacred of all.

My head now spinning, eyes blurring,

I could only hear screams.

I was blanking out from shock and pain,

blood spilling down my face, in streams.

I wanted this excruciating pain to end.

Just then, a boy stepped next to the huge man,

his silhouette shook me to my core – my friend?

I panicked and screamed,

"Leave, run, escape…"

But he simply gazed back at me,

and I saw fat tears running down his nape.

Ever so slowly, he loaded a giant heavy gun,

and it dawned on me –

although our childhood was common,

his had hidden an ugly story.

Our eyes met and we communicated.

Our entire friendship lay untranslated.

His tears tried hard to justify his grief,

and I understood him, strangely.

Urging him to push me,

into a world of painless relief.

Hands shivering vehemently,

he aimed his gun at me.

He pulled the trigger with a little push,

one bullet straight to my heart,

one more to my wobbling knee.

My last thought?

Of two little kids playing in the sands.

One four and the other – just three.

16. THE SILENT VOICE

I am not someone with big, blue eyes,

or cascading hair,

or lovely dimples,

or beauty that was rare.

I do not get my brows plucked,

or discuss how my day sucked.

I shy away from the camera,

I am not fun enough for the world.

I sit alone on the shore for hours together,

and lie on my couch, curled.

I do not adorn jewellery,

I hate fancy heels,

I walk around in baggy jeans –

For me, that heals.

I walk alongside people unknown,

I observe people more than some smartphone.

I do not have the latest iPhone,

nor the latest Kindle for "easy" reading,

I interact with a select few people and

find the smell of hard-bound books quite freeing.

I hardly visit pubs.

And I hate shopping.

I prefer sipping coffee on my patio,

over pub-hopping.

I do not easily befriend people,

but I do hold dear my own,

whose pictures you would certainly not find on my phone.

Some say I have a weird complex,

I say, "I agree".

You see, life has not been too fair with me,

and you may not, perhaps, disagree.

I lost my speech when I was two.

People would look at me with pity,

Treat me like another case of charity.

The fact that they had voices felt unfair.

I left myself alone, I hid my blues.

In the company of me and mine,

somehow, my silence found a voice too.

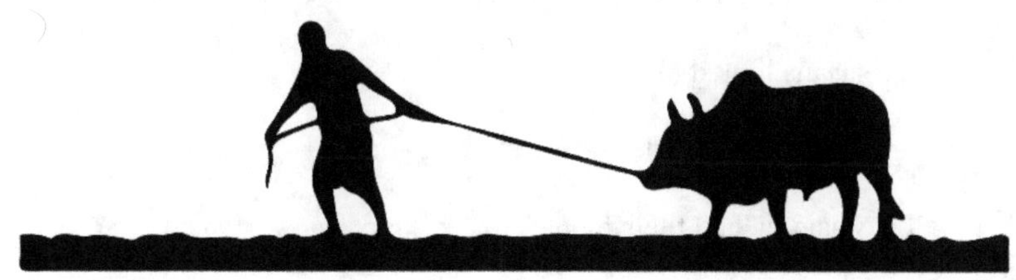

17. A MOO POINT

So many of us have no voice in the world's ways.

There is always someone to keep us in our place.

Why, are we not taught to believe –

for that what we do not deserve, we must not grieve?

Is there any difference between human beings and us, animals?

For, I have seen venomous people and sophisticated cannibals.

I once belonged to a farmer –

a father of four kids.

All naked and malnourished,

without a morsel of food.

While he toiled away in the fields,

barbarians looted his home,

yet, silently, he stood.

They said he had their money

and he said they had his land.

With passing time, however,

they always had more to demand.

Sometimes, he pleaded for mercy,

mostly, he stayed silent for years.

When they murdered his peers,

and finally, threatened to kill his family,

he was forced to seal his destiny.

He took me to an empty butcher's shop.

My dead body would earn him money.

My eyes met those of my master's,

and I felt the needle of time stop.

We spoke in silence,

unlike ever in the last five years.

A cow, just like a human,

has had no voice.

So, I bade him a farewell

mooing down his ears.

There is no difference between me and my master.

His silence brought on my death a little faster.

Our silences however beautiful and dutiful,

at knife point, our silences just become a 'moo' point.

18. PARADISE CALLING

I had promised my family a paradise forever.

But paradise was never to come cheap.

So, I left home, in search of ways better

to make money in heaps.

I made enough for a large mansion, towering minarets,

While all she just wanted was to hold my hands

and watch the sunsets.

I made more money – enough to take Mom on a cruise trip.

But all she wanted was to spend a day with me, roundtrip.

A little more I made for my kids and their kids,

but all they wanted were my bedtime stories

with the same old twists.

Alas, today, when I was finally headed home,

a bomb suddenly hit my village

and destroyed everything that I called my own.

My entire life flashed in front of my eyes.

All my promises felt like blurred lines and burnt lies.

Why did I ever come away?

I want those sunsets with my wife,

time with the kids – my whole life…

What choices made me play these cruel volleys?

Why, this irony?

When I had saved for a future,

my present was destroyed by time and its follies.

Had I not promised them a paradise forever?

A paradise that was timeless, ending never?

Just then, an alarm rang,

and I awoke,

startled, sweating.

Jesus, this was the worst nightmare,

my heart thudding and beating.

Was I not at the end of a three-year offshore meeting,

with only a few days left, before returning?!

I looked at my return tickets

and got packing, smiling.

Phew. I was heading home, finally.

My forever was now,

and my paradise was calling.

19. THOUGHTS

Some thoughts I want to hide,

Some thoughts I can only confide.

Thoughts there are, that can be rolled,

some, though, just cannot be controlled.

Some thoughts that are yet to crowd our mind,

to those thoughts, oh, dear heart, please be kind.

20. ALWAYS A NEW BEGINNING...

A tear trickled down her cheek,

as she watched him leave.

Would she ever see his face again?

She sat there in disbelief.

Mei's coffee lay untouched,

her heart starting to dissolve,

Their loud arguments fresh in her ears,

this time, without a resolve.

Far away, a football player lay on the ground,

fighting the agony of a nasty fall.

The final goal was "in his hands",

but one weak moment, and he had lost it all.

The crowd roared in pain.

Their groans and sighs –

Rio could hear it all.

Yet, he could not bring himself to open his eyes,

and watch his impending downfall.

Miles away, Phil watched their debut novel

lie around in the bookstore,

uncared for, unnoticed.

A book could not have failed more.

Buyers picked other books,

picked other people.

Should Phil ever write again?

The thought poked like a needle.

Along came a phoenix,

with eyes that soothed pain and wings that defined beauty.

With a message from the sun,

her light could cut through any sky sooty.

She asked them to open their distraught eyes,

to shed away their last tear.

The world would not stop for their sorrows,

they would have to change time's gear.

Mei ran towards the love of her life.

He was now walking away.

She held him by the scruff,

and asked him to stay.

If he left, there would be no reasons to fight,

or ones to make hay.

The phoenix brought Rio back to life,

He opened his eyes to his reality –

Wasn't his failure reason enough

to kick back alive?

Phil understood the phoenix' message.

They rushed to the store,

took the bundle of books galore,

ran to the nearest care home,

and distributed them to veterans, seniors and more.

Every fall taught them a lesson,
Every new start needed a reason.

At each of their lowest points,

they listened to the phoenix in their heart.

When their failures looked like "the end",

a phoenix helped turn it into a new start.

Each time they thought they were losing,

they were truly winning.

Like the sun that emerges from the clouds,

the phoenix inspired a new beginning.

21. THE JOURNEY THAT MATTERS

It does not matter,

what train we board,

our destinations,

old, new, battered, or unexplored.

It does not matter,

what seats we choose.

Sewn, torn,

some old, some new.

The train halts at different stations,

teach us new lessons of patience.

Just trust the people we travel with.

Just trust that our destination is not some myth.

Faces known, motives unknown,

Hearts of gold, some forlorn.

When the train finally stops, we look back,

at the many scenes and stops on our track.

It is then that we realize what truly matters,

Not the destination, not the dime.

For you, me, and all travellers of time,

it has always been the journey that matters.

22. YOU

So many places yearn for your eyes,

So many people long for your smile,

So much music awaits your ears,

So many moments worth joyful tears.

So much food you are yet to try,

Swap your feast with an other's rye.

So many nights full of bright, twinkling stars,

lie beyond the comfort of rushing cars.

Pause, walk, run, and jump high

to reach those milestones and touch that sky.

Hug that one person you never hugged in all these years,

or take a plunge and face your fears.

Pause, for a moment, shift your gears,

you are a lighthouse for many, a pier for peers.

Get out of your dark space,

Show us that raw face.

You have been cooped up all this while,

when so many have been longing for your smile.

An adventure, an entire story lies ahead.

So many undiscovered places to bring back from the dead.

Take a step forward, maybe some deep breaths.

For every breath you take clears that fog in your head.

There, you just got yourself some life-changing to do,

So, you would not give up on yourself just yet, would you?